BITTER SWEET VOICES

A Symphony of Echoes and Emotions

Simran Johal (PCS)

Dedication

"I dedicate this book to myself-for having the courage to take the first step in sharing the whispers of my heart with the world. May these poetic musings find a home in the hearts of those who read them."

Preface

Life is a symphony of emotions-a delicate interplay of joy and sorrow, hope and despair, silence and resilience. ***Bitter Sweet Voices*** is born from these very echoes, a collection of poetic musings that reflect the myriad emotions we encounter on our journey.

From the quiet strength of womanhood to the fragility of trust, from the fading hues of nature's canvas to the pursuit of endless joy, exploring the raw,unfiltered moments that shape us. The verses speak of kindness, of courage, of the void within, and the unyielding will to go on. Some poems may whisper, while others may roar, but all carry the weight of human experience—the voices we hear, the ones we silence, and those that refuse to fade. Within these pages also lie verses that drift into the *Elysium* of love, where love is nothing but love itself—just a pure and timeless emotion. And then there is a tender glance into childhood, a nostalgic embrace of fleeting memories—of a time when we longed to grow up too soon, only to realize, as the years pass, that all we wish for is to return to the innocence.

This collection also includes a special poem on *Shivaya—the eternal truth*, a reflection on the divine essence that transcends time and form. Additionally, it delves into the profound teachings of *Shri Guru Gobind Singh Ji* on the five vices —lust, anger, greed, attachment, and ego — from which these bittersweet voices are often born, yet against which the human spirit can triumph.

This book is an ode to every soul that has felt deeply, struggled silently, and, above all, learned the essence of true love—be it in its purest form, in self-discovery, or in the act of loving oneself before seeking it in the world. May these words resonate with you, offering comfort, reflection or simply the understanding that you are not alone in this ever-changing tide of emotions.

With Gratitude
Simran Johal

Acknowledgements

First and foremost, I express my deepest gratitude to the divine force that guides me—Lord Shiva, who has been an eternal reminder of the boundless completeness that pervades the universe, and to the wisdom of Shri Guru Gobind Singh Ji, a poet of profound brilliance who believed in the immense power of the pen and the enduring strength of ink. His words were not just verses but a force of courage, and truth, inspiring generations to rise beyond their struggles. Their presence in this collection is a humble tribute to the path of self-discovery and resilience.

This book is a piece of my heart, a collection of emotions woven into words, and bringing it to life would not have been possible without the love, support, and inspiration I have received along the way.

I am endlessly grateful to my family, whose unwavering belief in me has been my greatest strength. Your encouragement, patience, and love have been the foundation upon which these verses stand.

And above all, to the life experiences that have shaped me, challenged me, and inspired me to write these verses—thank you. Every moment, every encounter, and every emotion has played a part in crafting this collection. Without them, these Bittersweet Voices would have remained unheard.

Thank You
Simran Johal

SHIVAYA~ THE ETERNAL TRUTH

Shivaya is a pure Emotion
Shivaya is the inner devotion

Shivaya is the ultimate reality
Shivaya brings in the real stability

Shivaya transforms pain into pleasure
Shivaya turns the poison into nector's treasure

Shivaya is the path to the formless in every Essence
Shivaya is the presence in everything around and in every sense

Shivaya is the guide to Maa Parvati's penance and her endless love, longing to meet
Shivaya is the Ardhanarishwar manifestation of Shiva and Parvati as an ecstatic greet

Shivaya is the energy for Nandi's single pointed focus

and eternal wait
Shivaya is the a path to Nandi's true devotional gate

Shivaya is the eternal and infinite bliss
Shivaya is the way of life so be aware and never miss

To Shivaya let us all surrender in his divine energy
beyond our limited perception
To Shivaya Let's bow down and be open to his
pleasurable reception

OM NAMAH SHIVAYA
HAR HAR MAHADEV

Trust : A Mirage

Trust I pose in God as people change like seasons
You ask me as to why , Well ! I have my own reasons
Some say you overthink and some say you doubt
My friend, it was broken too often so which trust you
talk about ?
It takes a span to build and shattered with such ease
Trusting becomes an effort in this world of materialism
where majority just came to please

Womanhood

Look at her face
What a grace !
She looks as bright as the sun
To be around her is always fun

Look at her face what a zeal
Surrounded by love and compassion is her feel
She is filled with enthusiasm to work hard
And protects her loving one's like a guard

Look at her face how aspirational she looks
Whatever she sets her mind on to she achieves it by
hook or crook
Her ability to shine is what everyone love
Well it's her hands which not just support the cradle but
has the ability to rise above !

Look at her face ! Who is she ?
A daughter, mother, sister and wife

Womanhood she represents making everyone's life
bright
Like the strong branches holding everyone tight
She is a woman ! The strength of everyone and guiding
everyone right
She is a woman ! Fighting every wrong with a Smile on
her face and with all the might !

The will to Go one !

The will to go on must sustain
The Path wouldn't be free of pain

It may seem hard and it may seem tough
The beautiful journeys are usually rough

It may seem onerous and emotionally draining
But trust me my friend that's where you are actually
gaining

It may seem like grilling under the hot fire
Keep going with the same zeal until more higher you
aspire

You will win and reach the top
Keep going with spirit to succeed and never stop !

Faces of Silence

What does thy silence mean ? From where of thy silence
is born ?
Is it a feeling of the torn ?
Is it a lover's moment to adorn ?
Is it a precursor to a sea storm ?
From where of this silence is born ?

Silence is communication they say
Silence for the preacher is a path to pray
Silence for some is a joyous stay
Silence for the angry takes the anguish away

Silence for a dejected lover is the voice itself so loud
Silence for the lonely is the feeling of numbness in the
crowd

Silence is a women's hidden pain
It becomes forced as her voice she knows is all in vain

Silence for Mother Earth is a connection to the divine

Silence For the aesthetic is the authentic existence and a
reflection to shine

Silence for some is the realization of the righteous deed
Silence for the gluttonous is the inner voice to stop to his
greed

Some are in its continuous seek
Some consider it an expression of the meek
Some feel it makes you weak
For some it's the inner voice to reach the peak

Silence has manifestations of different kind
In its own ways its become a path to unwind

The pursuit of Endless Joy

Happiness around I look for, as hollow within I feel
The world's riches are mine to own, within I have no zeal
Lost in its pursuit, away from melancholy, how can I
within heal ?
Is happiness a distant path or is it a timeless feel ?

Listen ! Why chase it, why are you on the run ?
In the pursuit of material goals have you forgotten the
fun ?

Why don't you calm down and stop this emotional gush
Stop, pause and reflect my friend, why are you in a rush
?

Achievement driven happiness is what you search
Happiness is this very moment itself, Wait ! let your
emotions perch

Away from the noise, within 'I' and 'You' it prevail
Its the gift from the divine, that lets the human's sail

Look within and not around, for in the tiniest speck it is
found
Gaze inside and witness it's presence profound
You are joy itself, pure and unbound
Let it bloom, for in every particle of yours it is found

Nature's Fading Canvas

Those churping voices of the birds and the divinely
echoes
The lush green trees and nature's ethos

The dew drops on the petals when fall
The vibrant serenity makes me stall

The butterfly giving winks to the flowers
The drizzles kissing the trees with heavenly showers

The peacock's radiating their vibrant sides
Their dance to the rain being an expression of fides

The bliss of pristine nature if untouched, would to
humans be Mother Earth's shade
Why see it degrade O ye people ?, Don't let the canvas
fade !

Let's stand strong and protect it through our deeds
Don't let it become a debt for future generations so use it

wisely with minimalist needs

Let's protect the Nature's Canvas for the World ahead
Why see its colours fade and do our bit instead !

Calling the Inner Courage

People say the world lacks kindness today,
I say it's courage in unity that's gone astray

People say they are impaired to the injustice happening
around,
I say you don't have the courage to fight, to your
limitations you are bound

People say we don't see love around,
I say you have lost the courage to love profound

People say the world is scattering with cleavages of
different kind,
I say because you have lost the courage to be of open
mind

People say the world is driven by betrayals and hate,
I say you have lost the courage to have faith in the
human mate

Let not the evils of selfishness, anger, materialism and
lust shake your courage,
let's build a peaceful world which is kind
Let's call out love with open arms and let our affection
unwind

The Ocean of Kindness

The heart is kind
When selflessness is blind
When Love is enshrined in your mind
Well ! Let's give it a thought how often this kindness we
find

The lust for materialism is what prevails
Come what may for my interest I would trail
The compassion seems to have taken a back seat, where
the human beings fail
Well ! Let's give it a thought how this ocean of lust we
would sail

Let love be our guiding light
Certainly into a peaceful world it would be a wonderful
flight
Let not this hunger of selfishness break you, Come one !
Hold your hands tight
Well ! Let's give it a thought and fight it with all the
might

Well ! Let's give it a thought and make this world look
even bright !

16

GURU GOBIND SINGH JI's
Way TO LIFE

As we walk the path in our lives, concoction of emotions
we face
Let's go by the the directions under GURU GOBIND Ji's
grace

ANGER if thy face, the rhythmic movement of heart
goes high
Act with composure and take a deep sigh

Let not the PRIDE take over your sense
Let humbleness be your fence

Why ATTACH to the material illusion ?
In the name of GOD let your attachment be surrendered
under a divine fusion

Let not the LUST turn you blind
Wait ! Listen to the conscious voice and be kind

GREEDS have made the mighty fall
Let Dasvandh as per REHITNAMAS be your moral call

Let not these evils take over your emotions to act in
Potential State
Be in the State of Equipoise guided by your OWN will
and see the miracles await

Walk the path of Dharma and make the righteous
choices
Listen to the compassion filled Divine's nectar and not
the Bitter Sweet Voices

The Real You

The real me or the real you !
Who are you - What is true ?

You wear many faces each passing day,
Leaving behind traces along the way.

Some see you as innocent and free,
A playful soul, full of glee.

Yet to others, you're sharp and wise,
A clever mind in disguise.

Some call you a leader strong,
Guiding others, lighting the way along.

To some, you're loving and deep,
A heart that takes a lover's leap.

Some witness you as a fiery one,
The force that helps you get things done.

Others may call you envious too,
But don't let that shadow define you.

Some see kindness in all you do,
A soul so pure, loyal, and true.

So which one is your true face ?
To me it's a maze when I have a gaze.

Which one is you or your face ?
Well ! We all wear masks in this life's race.

The Drowning Me

In that corner alone I stood
What do I do little I understood

The anxious me couldn't comprehend
A smiling face to the world I pretend

Pushing myself everyday but I couldn't walk
You can do it, to myself I talk

Whom to tell, whom to speak I couldn't find
How easy would it be if the world around us was a
little kind

Judgement, Fear and Envy all around
It feels they are the pulling shackles with which I am
bound

My heart needs a vent to let my voice out
I need a love filled rain and not an emotionless drought

Is Someone there who would listen my heart out
It would heal me inside without a doubt

For now alone I stood as I look around
Hold me up before I am drowned

Woman- Not a Caged Parrot

They dictate my entire life
From the womb to being a wife

They kill me in the womb
They built with their own hands my tomb
But why ? Because I am a daughter

They tell me what to do and what to wear
They tell me these are your limits you can't go there
But why ! Because I am a women

Well ! it continues as I grow
They say get married and do this with their dictated flow
!
But why ? Because I am a grown women

As I proceed and leave my parent's house
As I become a wife married to my spouse

This doesn't stop and goes ahead
He calls me his property and the relationship being
patriarchy led

Well ! To these shackles, freedom they proudly acclaim
Anything wrong done to a girl it's her blame

She is raped, harassed and not given wings to fly
Let her breathe open from being a Caged parrot and
she'll touch the sky !

Give her the due share which she deserves
As it's the Civilizations that a women preserves

Love Thyself

Love thyself before you loose
Only and only yourself you should choose

In this life's race, we forgo who we really are
You are you ! Remember you are a shining star

The shine in the others brightness fades you away
You are you ! Let your shine stay

You are the best version of the creation
You are you ! You are a God's celebration

You might feel low in some set norms
You are you ! Everyone has their different forms

Why run the race and set for yourself these standard
bars
You are you ! Don't live just for others, it'll give you
deep scars

You change for love, why my friend ?
You are you ! True love comes with acceptance of flaws
so why fit in this trend

You are the best in your body type
You are you ! So be you and don't t be a part of the hype

Some will like and some would hate
You and you ! For you are great

Don't fear that something you'll loose
You are you ! If have a choice, only You and You should
you choose

Let your true self love shine bright
Don't let yourself whither away in the false reality of the
crowd, hold yourself tight

You are worthy of the best of the world
Be who you are don't in the flock be furled

Don't forgo who you really are !
You are you ! And a bright and shining star

The Void Within

I feel the void within, it's for real and true
Only the self knows within, on the outside you have no
clue

They see me smile and achieve
This void they would never believe

The face I carry within, Well ! you hardly know
The void is real and makes me feel too low

I tried to ask why this void and is it really my fault ?
Trust me ! It's a silent assault

Some Understood and some listened to it a Pseudo way
How do I explain this feeling so with my emotions they
don't play ?

They say you become reticent and should be open
around
I want to share my heart out but someone true I hardly

found

Some say go with the flow and it's a mere thought
I know the invisible scar it gives, as all alone it was me
who against it fought

This helplessness makes me feel hollow
Where do I go and which path do I follow ?

Listen ! Listen to someone's emotional void and feel
It could be best antidote with which they could heal

The pittish feeling is real, so be an ear to someone, this is
my heartfelt appeal
This can be a turning point to make them live a life filled
with zeal

Elysium of Love

Unconditional love, isn't this itself a precondition ?
Love should be just love and with no ambition

Let love be like a river's gentle touch nurturing the
lover's path with affection
Embracing love with a flow deepening the soul's
connection

It's the journey to fall in love with the beloved's flaws
It's the journey to uplift the other with love filled
applause

It's not love at first sight, it may be so for some !
But it is the rose like blush everyday as if it's just begun

It's holding the hands as the sun sets
It's the growing warmth each day as older one gets

If one stumbles, it's the love which holds the other in the
arms and makes one rise like dawn

The love makes you realize the beauty it holds and to
deeper meaning one is drawn

It's the spiritual journey of the two souls as into one they
blend
Universe being the witness to this Elysium as they
transcend

Love is a state itself, it's the timeless feel like the oceanic
flow
Hence why call it unconditional or conditional ? For real
love is just Love entwined into an eternal glow !

The Illusional Mind

You think it's real but it is not
You experience it to be real but it is just a thought

The mind plays and tests your vulnerability in every way
Fear, loneliness, hallucinations and what not you
experience everyday

Those continuous voices and thoughts makes you
crumble so bad
You feel the rush to escape as the feeling within makes
you mad

What is it ? Is it for the real but difficult to prove
The mental health draining you from within and on your
heart making a deep groove

Fear induced actions in your every move
It's the monster's voice in the mind, how to the world I
prove ?

Fear not my friend you'll sail this emotional storm
And to the world now ! Mental health is for real so be
kind and warm

Act and Fear no Wrong

I fear no rightful wrong
For I am God's child and strong
Mistakes are the learnings and the journey is long
With every mistake I come up strong, I come up strong

Action form the the pedestal of the journey ahead
Each step with patience act like a connecting thread
What would be the result I leave it to God and I walk
through all my fears instead
To toil hard and intense is the Mantra with which I am
lead

Towards my Goal as I proceed
To act towards it is my deed
No wrong or right, a lesson follows with it indeed
To go on with persistence is my only Feed

The cost of doing nothing is more than cost of being
wrong
So act like Herculean and be strong

Let your action be a pleasant song
Driven by faith keep going with vision along
With every mistake I come up strong, I come up strong !

The Childhood Glance

I want to run back to my childhood if I had a chance
Well ! It's was the best one let's have a glance

It was all innocence that I had
A smiling face even if things were bad

From learning to sit to crawling to stand
To walking independent from walking hand in hand

The school marked the new dawn
Books, pencils and erasers? I look for them, where have
they gone?

The teenage hits with new talks
Presuming to be grown women with sparkling walks

Where it was all playful and vibrant around
I want to wrap it in my arms but it can't be found

The Chocolates, Toffees were a great treat

No judgements whether the luxuries or the streets

Where friendships were just so pure
To the sadness, the love filled laughters were the cure

Give me the Geography, History and Annual Plays back
Is there a code with which my Childhood I could hack

Where the school canteen was at par
It was indeed, life's best phase and matched no five star

The urge to grow old back then indeed very strong
As we grow old we realize, that we were actually wrong

Time waits for None and only the memories of
childhood stays
Make the best of every moment and create your own
beautiful plays

www.ingramcontent.com/pod-product-compliance
Lightning Source LLC
LaVergne TN
LVHW021310200726
843509LV00012B/1858